PEOPLE IN DELIVERY

BY
SHALINI VALLEPUR

BookLife PUBLISHING

©2022
BookLife Publishing Ltd.
King's Lynn
Norfolk PE30 4LS, UK

All rights reserved.
Printed in Poland.

A catalogue record for this book is available from the British Library.

ISBN: 978-1-80155-468-8

Written by:
Shalini Vallepur

Edited by:
John Wood

Designed by:
Jasmine Pointer

All facts, statistics, web addresses and URLs in this book were verified as valid and accurate at time of writing. No responsibility for any changes to external websites or references can be accepted by either the author or publisher.

Image Credits

All images are courtesy of Shutterstock.com, unless otherwise specified. With thanks to Getty Images, Thinkstock Photo and iStockphoto.

Cover – antoniodiaz, Gorodenkoff, SpeedKingz, Juliasart, alazur. 4–5 – LP2 Studio, Monkey Business Images. 6–7 – M_Agency, Gorodenkoff. 8–9 – alazur, rlat, Kauka Jarvi, Anatolir. 10–11 – Halfpoint, Gorodenkoff, Zeynur Babayev. 12–13 – May_Chanikran, B.Zhou, H.Elvin. 14–15 – Phoderstock, Bjoern Wylezich, alazur, ideyweb. 16–17 – pcruciatti, Drazen Zigic, YummyBuum. 18–19 – natashanast, Jaromir Chalabala, Avigator Fortuner, Photomarine, Tartila, freshcare. 20–21 – Atstock Productions, Daisy Daisy, LoopAll, Kunturtle, TaMih, Oxy_gen, jehsomwang. 22–23 – Sensvector, iceink, NTL studio, v74.

CONTENTS

Page 4	Here to Help
Page 6	People in Delivery
Page 8	At the Post Office
Page 10	At the Mail Centre
Page 12	Working at a Warehouse
Page 14	On the Road
Page 16	Out for Delivery!
Page 18	The Sea and the Sky
Page 20	Local Delivery
Page 22	Signed, Sealed, Delivered
Page 24	Glossary and Index

Words that look like **this** can be found in the glossary on page 24.

HERE TO HELP

There are lots of jobs in the world and each one is different. Some jobs are always needed. The people who do these jobs are called key workers.

Key can sometimes mean needed and important.

Teachers are always needed to teach us.

Without key workers, we would not have the things we need to live safely, such as food and important **services**.

PEOPLE IN DELIVERY

Have you ever sent a letter or **received** a parcel? People who work in delivery jobs are key workers. We need them to post letters, parcels and important **goods** such as food.

Lots of people work in delivery to make sure everything is received safely and on time. Let's learn about the different people and jobs in delivery!

AT THE POST OFFICE

When a letter is put into a post box, a postal worker goes to collect it. The postal worker may collect post from many post boxes in one day.

Large letters and parcels must be sent at a post office. Some postal workers sort through the letters and parcels, while others take them away to be delivered.

AT THE MAIL CENTRE

Post arrives at a big mail centre. Machines sort the post and parcels into groups depending on where they need to go. Workers make sure nothing goes wrong.

Forklift drivers use forklifts to carry post and other heavy goods around the mail centre. They help to load the post and goods onto lorries and vans.

WORKING AT A WAREHOUSE

A warehouse is a large building that has lots of goods inside. Some shops and supermarkets keep all their goods in warehouses. When they need the goods, they ask for them to be delivered.

Warehouse workers work hard each day and night to make sure everybody gets what they need. They check that the goods are going to the right place.

ON THE ROAD

Lorry drivers drive the goods closer to where they need to be delivered. Post and goods may be taken to other mail centres where they are checked and sorted by workers again.

When everything is sorted, the post is ready to be collected by postal workers and sent out for delivery.

15

OUT FOR DELIVERY!

Postal delivery workers collect post from a mail centre to deliver it. Each postal delivery worker has their own round. This means they may go to the same area every day to deliver post.

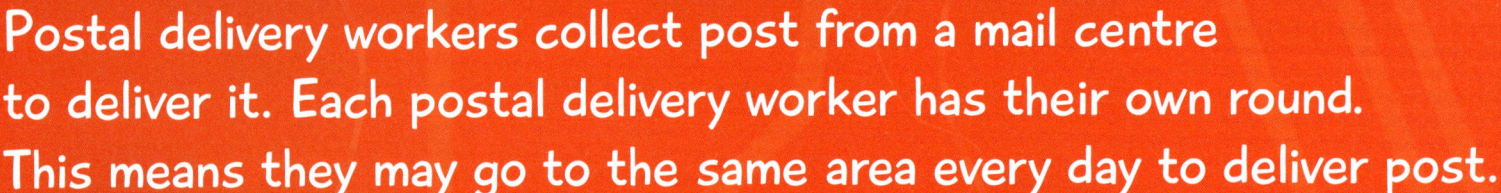

Some postal delivery workers deliver post and parcels by walking. Others may drive cars, vans or ride a bike.

Postal delivery workers deliver our post even when it's raining and snowing.

THE SEA AND THE SKY

Some goods are flown **overseas** on **cargo** planes. Workers pack and load the goods onto the plane, which is flown by a pilot.

Some post and goods need to be sent overseas on cargo ships. Workers load the goods into shipping containers which are lifted onto cargo ships.

Shipping containers

LOCAL DELIVERY

Some shops may deliver to people who live nearby. Many supermarkets can deliver fresh food straight to people's houses. Supermarket delivery vans are built to keep food cold.

Some restaurants and takeaways deliver cooked food. Delivery drivers collect the food from the restaurant or takeaway and take it straight to people's houses.

SIGNED, SEALED, DELIVERED

People all over the world work hard to make sure post is delivered on time. Next time you post something, think about how many people will help to deliver it.

Now you know all about some of the people who work in delivery! Can you match each job below with the right person?

Post office worker	Forklift driver	Postal delivery worker
Sorts post at a post office	Drives a forklift that lifts heavy things	Delivers post on rounds

GLOSSARY

cargo — things that are being transported by a ship or plane

goods — objects that people want and buy, such as food, computers, clothes and toys

overseas — to a different country, usually one that is across an ocean or sea

received — to have gotten

services — tasks or actions that people pay other people to do, such as caring for older people, fixing things that are broken or cleaning

INDEX

bikes 17
forklifts 11, 23
lorries 11, 14

mail centres 10–11, 14, 16
planes 18
post boxes 8

post offices 9, 23
ships 19
vans 11, 17, 20